Why Husbands should clean the Bathrooms!

Why Husbands should clean the Bathrooms!

S. Miller

SAM Publishing

Contents

First Printing, 2023

1

Prelude

Why Husbands Should Clean the Bathroom!

I had been married for 14 years and during that time I cleaned the bathroom countless times. I had thought, naively, that we were just dividing out the duties and it just so happened that cleaning the bathrooms fell in my lap. I would soon learn that this just was not the case.

Typically speaking, we would have people visiting so we had to do a deeper cleaning than normal. My wife said she would vacuum, dust, mop the floor, and pick up anything that needed to be put away etc., and I would clean the bathrooms. I thought this was a fair division of duties, and maybe slightly in my favor, so I always agreed. Over time, in various discussions with friends and acquaintances, I learned that when preparing for company they too were put in charge of cleaning the bathrooms. I soon learned of more and more husbands that were tasked with cleaning the bathrooms while their wives would do the bulk of the rest of the cleaning.

But why? Why would the wives be so willing to do most of the other cleaning in exchange for husbands cleaning the bathrooms AND without complaining?! Is it because they figure they do most of the cleaning anyway? Is it because they are much more particular about how to clean the rest of the house? I'm sure these reasons play into it to some degree, but it still doesn't add up! Could it be that they figure we do so much other work around the house that they just give us a small job to help out? HA! HA! HAAAaaaa! Ok. Ok.. back to reality! Well, the only explanation that I could come up with is that... **women hate cleaning bathrooms!**

Why bathrooms, as opposed to kitchens, teenagers' bedrooms, or basements, which can be just as filthy at times? My only theory is that they cannot stand the thought of cleaning up someone else's urine! Let me explain, being male myself, I can attest to the fact that occasionally, and I stress occasionally, I do miss the intended target! This is not intentional at all! In fact as a young boy you look for targets within the toilet itself to "shoot" at to hone in your sharp shooting skills. Now being a responsible mature male adult, at least in theory, I will immediately clean it up with some toilet paper. However, young males and small boys especially, tend not to clean up after the misfire.

It is my belief that wives think that since there is no possible way the urine that finds its way to the floor around the base of the toilet cannot possibly be theirs. The only way this happens is via the male species of the household. Since the husband is the head male of the household he should be the one to clean the bathrooms.

Now, I have never heard a woman admit to this, but it must be what they are thinking... **I just know it!** They completely disregard the fact that there is make-up, lotion, and various other ointments, smeared all over the vanity. They completely ignore the fact that there are long strands of hair all over the place, which for most husbands I know is just a constant reminder of what they are lacking!

But in their mind since there is no way in **hell** that the little bit of urine that finds its way to the floor can be theirs, therefore, the **husbands must clean the bathrooms!!**

This is where I come in. There is no use in trying to fight this way of thinking. It is a losing battle. Trust me on this one. So, what is a husband to do? My solution is, rather than fighting it, make it work for you! If you follow the recommendations I lay out in the following chapters, I see it as a win-win situation. In fact, if you follow my suggestions and "clean" the bathrooms for your wives I am willing to bet that your wife will be more than just glad you cleaned the bathroom she will be ecstatic! In most cases an ecstatic wife is a willing wife if you know what I mean! That's right! She may even let you go golfing with the guys once the company leaves!

FORE!

2

The Definition of Clean

The definition of "clean" is vital to making this whole "cleaning of the bathroom" work. Without a full and complete grasp of the definition of "clean" all the effort and good intentions will go down the toilet! (Yes, the pun was intended)

The key thing to remember here is that men and women have a different idea of what "clean" is. If you don't believe me just compare a guy's dorm room to a girl's dorm room, or a bachelor's house to a bachelorette's house.

A man's definition is simple and straightforward. If it looks clean and it smells clean, it must be clean. Seems to be a very logical and sensible approach, however, therein lies the problem. Logic and common sense have nothing to do with a woman's definition of "clean." Wives, before you start sending disparaging comments let me try and explain myself.

As far as I can tell a woman's definition of clean is the following: **Looks clean + smells clean + feels clean + time = clean.**

The way I see it, is that if you clean the bathroom and it looks clean, smells clean, but only took you 5 minutes to clean it, it will not be acceptable to your wife. She will be thinking that it cannot be possible to clean it in that short amount of time no matter how clean it looks and smells. In fact, she is most likely thinking if she had to clean it herself, she would spend a minimum 20-30 minutes just on cleaning up the urine, that no way in hell she should have to clean. By the way she thinks of all this in less than a tenth of a second.

You could have it so clean that it would be approved to perform surgery in there but if it only took 5 minutes it is not acceptable! If you dare argue with her, or shall I say, suggest in any way shape or form that she is mistaken and that in fact it really is clean, she will go to great lengths to show you that not only is it not clean, but it is in fact still filthy!

She will look underneath the backside of the toilet where no one has seen since the toilet was installed just to show you that it is not clean. She will look inside the vanity back behind the sink and point out a tiny spider web just to prove that it is not clean. She will do whatever it takes to show that it is not clean so do not even bother to fight this battle. I repeat, for your health and the overall well-being of your family and marriage, do not fight this battle! You will lose every time! Just resign yourself to the fact that time is a key element to a woman's definition of "clean." I will explain how to address this situation in a later chapter.

The "feeling factor" is a little tougher to get a handle on and can vary from woman to woman. Basically, if the bathroom looks clean, smells clean, and a lot of time was spent on cleaning it, but it does not "feel" clean to them...it is not clean! How might this be you ask? Well, let's say in cleaning the bathroom you used a lot of Lysol spray, bleach products, etc., and in showing her how clean you got the bathroom you turn on all the lights. You do this because of course you are proud of how clean the bathroom is, however, when she steps in she doesn't like it because it doesn't "feel" clean or make her feel good. It feels too much like a hospital and therefore is not "clean" in her eyes.

Of course, we are thinking that hospitals are very clean so isn't that a good thing? Trust me, do **not** go there, especially you newly married youngsters. The husbands that have been married for a while know of what I speak. It seems to be a logical thought and argument. Hospitals are clean so if it is like a hospital that is a good thing, right? Wrong! Must I remind you that logic has nothing to do with a woman's definition of clean!

In her mind it goes something like the following: "If it is like a hospital and hospitals have sick and dying people in them why on God's green earth would anyone in their right mind want their bathroom to make their guests think of sick and dying people! Now if you can't seem to understand this I guess I will have to do it myself just like I have to do everything else around here!" Again, this thought process takes her less than a tenth of a second if that. So just like with the "time" element you must resign yourself to the fact that it must also feel clean to be clean. It is just another argument that there is no hope in winning.

Now, after learning the differences in the definition of clean, you might be thinking that if you do clean the bathrooms you have gotten the short end of the deal since it will end up being more work and time than doing all the other cleaning chores combined. That is exactly how the wives think you should think...I think? Understanding this is the key in making this whole bathroom thing work out to your advantage all the while keeping her ecstatic about how clean the bathroom is. Remember, if logic is not a part of a woman's definition of clean you must use that to your advantage! Read on!

3

The Setup

There are two key elements in the set up that will go a long way to achieving the win-win situation of a "clean" bathroom. If logic is not in a woman's definition of clean then it goes to reason that it does not necessarily have to be clean to be "clean" if you get my drift! The first part of the set up is giving her the perception that a lot of time was spent on cleaning the bathroom. Remember basically in her mind it is virtually impossible to spend too much time cleaning the bathroom and that no matter how much time you spend in cleaning a bathroom it just may still not be enough!

So, giving her the perception that a lot of time was spent cleaning becomes a win-win situation. You do not actually have to spend a lot of time cleaning the bathroom but if she thinks you did you will be giving her the peace of mind that ultimately is what she is really after.

The other element of the setup is giving the impression that cleaning the bathroom is an arduous task at best. The harder she perceives it is to clean the bathroom "properly" the more thankful she will be that you are cleaning them. Shall I say she may even be ecstatic about it! Start cleaning those clubs now!

The "time" set-up goes something like this. You must listen to your wife (I know this can be hard but it will be worth it, trust me on this), to find out when she will be running to the store, or other errands, to get whatever. If she does not plan on going to the store for anything, you must come up with a reason for her to go. One idea is you can say to her something like, "we should really have some red wine on hand because I think that's what (insert guest's name) likes and I need to get started on cleaning the bathrooms so if you wouldn't mind…". The key thing here is that you ask for something for the guest since if you say you need something for yourself the chances of her agreeing to go get it diminish greatly.

The point of having her go to the store is to give the impression that the job takes much longer than it really will. So, you can sit there and watch the game or whatever but when she goes to grab her coat or gives any hint that she will be leaving soon you start hauling cleaning materials to the bathroom and I mean hauling. Part two of the set up is to give the impression that it is a monumental task to clean the bathroom. Bring bottles of all kinds of cleaners, mops, broom, and a good supply of rags and towels (you will need a bunch more when you actually do the cleaning which will be explained more in the next chapter). Right before she is about to leave you haul all this stuff to the bathroom but do not put it in the bathroom it must be in the hallway where she can see it and has to walk around it to get through. If she doesn't see it, she will not get the full impact of how much of a job this really is. 😉

The presence of a lot of cleaners is not enough, however, to maximize this impression of a huge task. The dirtier the bathroom is before cleaning, the harder it must be to clean, right? So, starting that morning you must do a few things to accomplish this. If you have kids this will already be accomplished for you with the kids bathroom since they are great at messing up bathrooms. For the bathrooms that they do not use you can do the following.

Brush your teeth and flick your toothbrush at the mirror to get that messed up a bit, shave with an electric razor and get beard shavings all over the counter, and smear toothpaste or some ointment on all chrome to take away from the shine. Remember shine equals clean and no shine equals dirty. Then the last thing to do, and hopefully you drank a lot of coffee in the morning, is to take plenty of time sitting on the throne (hint: remember to keep the fan off). Remember, bad smell equals not clean. The key is the dirtier it appears the cleaner it will appear even if a half-ass job was done cleaning it!

Once the setup is complete and your wife leaves for the store you will have to do "the cleaning", which will be explained in the next chapter. The cleaning should not take more than 10 minutes per bathroom. To finish the impression of time, on the last bathroom just leave a small spot on the floor that still needs to be wiped up. The best spot would be right by the door. Then go finish watching the game until you hear the garage door go up, or her car door close, and go back to the bathroom. For the best effect get on your knees and wipe up the last spot or two on the floor when your wife is looking. Being on the knees gives the impression of harder work!

The last thing to do is to haul all the cleaning materials back, making sure she sees you doing most of this. It will have accomplished the impression that you have been working very hard the whole time she was gone, which will go a long way in fulfilling the time factor in the "clean" equation. And now, of course, you can go back to watching the game since you have been working **so** hard and all the bathrooms are clean!

4

The Cleaning

Efficiency is the key to cleaning the bathroom, after all the whole point of this is to make the bathroom look, smell, and feel clean with the least amount of effort but get credit for doing a major project. Just to get any other thoughts out of your mind, as far as how you can accomplish this, I will tell you up front that the use of a high pressure washer may initially seem to be very quick and efficient but the lack of a floor drain, among other things, makes it a bit too impractical. Just saying.

The first thing you must consider is the smell. By trial and error, you need to find a scented cleaner and air freshener spray that your wife likes. I recommend staying away from any pine smelling cleaners since they do not seem to cover all the odors adequately and may end up making the bathroom smell like somebody did their business in the woods!

The first step is to take everything out of the bathroom and make sure you have lots of rags and towels on hand. For the next step you need to take the dust buster and suck up everything that is not nailed down or a shop vac if you prefer! This is much quicker than sweeping and a dustpan. The following step is to use the toilet bowl cleaner, so put a shi* ton (pun intended) of it in, on, and around the toilet. I figure wherever the urine goes so should the cleaner. Also, if a bunch gets on the floor don't worry, it will only help clean it! It stands to reason that if it is strong enough to clean a toilet it should be great for cleaning the floor. Take the toilet brush and scrub the inside of the toilet so fast that you get a good whirlpool going, so much so that it spills out onto the floor. Scrub with the brush the sides and the floor where it all spilled. By the time you are done cleaning the toilet you will be half done with the floor already!

Now get a bucket of hot water, with the cleaner you determined smelled the best, and using a big rag just wipe everything down. I mean everything, the mirror, vanity, shower, and whatever else looks like it could use it. Make sure you slop it on heavy so it is dripping on the floor, which will help clean that as well. Remember, the more the cleaner is spread around the more it will get a cleaner smell going. Then take several real big towels and dry everything except the floor.

Use plenty of dry towels, think of a car wash where they dry the whole car in a matter of seconds. The key to this is dry towels. When you are done with the towels throw them in the wash machine along with the rags you used, turn it on and forget about them. When she discovers all those towels and rags in the wash machine it will emphasize the extent at which you went to clean these bathrooms! So do not worry about how many towels you use. At this point you should have spent no more than 5 minutes.

When it comes to clean, shine is always good, and that bring us to the glass/chrome step of cleaning the bathroom. A quick spray of glass cleaner on all the chrome and glass then a quick wipe down with yet another clean dry rag should do the trick. If for some reason this does not do the trick on the chrome due to a build up of crud from the lack of using decent cleaners in the past I would suggest looking to the garage. The way I see it most guys have all kinds of stuff to make and keep their cars looking good and shiny so you must have something that will work on the bathroom chrome. I might suggest some chrome wheel cleaner. Again, the way I see it is if it is strong enough to clean your tire rims it has to be plenty good to clean anything in the bathroom. (Author disclaimer...if you do use chrome wheel cleaner, I claim no responsibility if it wrecks anything! It may be that you just have cheap faucets!)

We are now on the last leg of the cleaning process. All that needs to be done is to take, yes, yet another big dry towel and dry the floor. You might say hey I did not even scrub it but you must remember at this point in time there should be close to an inch of water and cleaner on the floor already so in the drying process you will be in essence scrubbing it as well. It doesn't get any more efficient that that!

If this is the last bathroom, which should be the one closest to where your wife may see you cleaning when she gets home, leave a small spot on the floor to wipe up when she is watching. You should also have all the other cleaners and materials, that you may or may not have used, at this bathroom as well to be put away just after she gets home. Now, all you do is spray the air freshener in the 3 key strategic areas. The first is behind the toilet, the second is in the shower area, and third by the vanity.

This concludes the cleaning portion and should not have taken more than 10 minutes per bathroom. If you find that it does take longer, I am confident with some time and practice you should not have a problem accomplishing this.

5

The "Feel" Factor

Before we go any further let's review the woman's definition of "clean" and see where we stand at this point. **Looks clean + smells clean + time + feelings = clean.** Chapter 4 took care of the "looks clean" and "smells clean" and the set up from chapter 3 account for the "time" factor. So, we are right on schedule with only feeling clean yet to take care of.

I can sum up the feeling factor in one word, **ambiance**. After all it is ambiance that makes a woman want to go to the most expensive restaurants instead of the local diner. It may be the same food, but it just "feels" like it tastes and looks better when you have the "ambiance".

The two key elements to setting the right ambiance is a dimmer switch and scented candles. Of course, the dimmer switch is something that will need to be installed as soon as possible. I would suggest right after you get done reading this book. In fact, finish your business, pull up your drawers, and go do it now!! You can finish reading this book when your done with this project and by then you probably will have to go to the bathroom again anyways. For you guys that use the google machine to find a handyman to do work around the house make the call now and get back to reading the rest of the book.

The dimmer switch is key for two reasons. First it is great for setting the mood, again fine restaurants do not have bright lights in the dining area, it is always dimmed lighting. Remember in the beginning of the book I stated that if you make it so bright and shiny it may make it "feel" like you're in a hospital. The dimmer switch will solve this potential problem.

The second, and just as important, reason for the dimmer switch is that the low lighting will make it hard to see any of the missed spots that maybe did not get as clean as they should have. This is what will make the difference between finishing the bathroom in 10 minutes or taking way too much time! If you know you have the dimmer switch to rely on you will be able to go faster and say to yourself at each step of the cleaning process, " Ah good enough!"

By now I am sure you know what the candles are for. Yes, that is right, they are the icing on the cake for setting the "mood". If you have used the right fragranced cleaner and air refresher, have dimmed lighting, and top it off with a good scented candle, your wife will be so thrilled with the "feel" of the bathroom that it won't even cross her mind to check to see how clean you "really" got it. In fact, she may be so thrilled that not only will she let you go golfing with your buddies after the guests leave, she may even provide you with a little "sugar" when you get home, if you know what I mean. That's right she may have some freshly baked chocolate chip cookies waiting for you when you get home!! It doesn't get any better than that!

6

Conclusion

Well guy's what do you think? Was I right about why you should clean the bathrooms? The way I see it, it's a win-win situation. You do not spend a whole lot of time cleaning the bathrooms but end up getting major credit for doing so, i.e. golf and chocolate chip cookies! Your wife wins because she just wants the bathrooms to be "clean" by her definition and if it looks clean, smells clean, feels clean, and took plenty of "time" to do it therefore it is clean. Right?!

Now, I know what you may be thinking... what if my wife reads this book. Well, I would say that what all marriages need to succeed is a little give and take. So, if you have read this whole book, (I am referring to you, the wives) just remember **URINE AROUND THE TOILETS!**

If after reading this book you no longer want him to "clean" the bathrooms, then that only leaves you to do it! My advice is to pretend you never read this book and just enjoy the fact that you will never have to clean the bathrooms and contend with the dreaded urine around the toilets ever again. Remember your own definition of clean? You cannot tell me with a straight face that you would not thoroughly enjoy a bathroom that has dimmed lighting, a scented candle, and smells great! So do not get hung up on how it got that way just enjoy the fact that it is that way. See what I mean, it truly is a win-win situation for husband and wife and can go a long way in helping you have that oh so allusive great marriage that many have searched for but never find. Just remember that all great marriages begin in, with, around, the toilet, or I dunno but you get the idea!

Note: Wives if you have indeed read this whole book and are going to follow my advice of pretending you didn't, do not forget to reward your husband for the great job he has done. That will help keep everything working like a well-oiled machine! Well, I have to get a glass of milk, now, to wash down my cookies.

I hope you enjoyed the book and I wish you many "clean" bathrooms in the future.

www.ingramcontent.com/pod-product-compliance
Lightning Source LLC
Chambersburg PA
CBHW050746150726
48196CB00004B/361

* 9 7 9 8 2 1 8 0 7 2 6 4 3 *